REDEMPTION
FROM
WITHIN

ADJUSTING THE AFRICAN MENTALITY

IFEANYICHUKWU UKO

authorHOUSE®

AuthorHouse™
1663 Liberty Drive
Bloomington, IN 47403
www.authorhouse.com
Phone: 1 (800) 839-8640

Published by AuthorHouse 02/15/2018

ISBN: 978-1-5462-2978-0 (sc)
ISBN: 978-1-5462-2976-6 (hc)
ISBN: 978-1-5462-2977-3 (e)

Library of Congress Control Number: 2018902200

Print information available on the last page.

REDEMPTION FROM WITHIN CONTENT

PREFACE

This novel titled 'Redemption from Within' is aimed at awakening the conscience of we Africans, including my beloved African American brothers and sisters and most especially Nigerians. Having lived at least a decade in both the west-African country of Nigeria and in the United States of America, I have witnessed great potential from we Africans, alas, the manifestations in African countries and most African-American communities display pitiful realities.

I have decided to focus on the African minds on this piece, because the status of our situation is critical. It is now the year 2018, and in this modern age, we as Africans are still struggling to get the basic things right.

Many children in Africa still go hungry, even worse, starving; a significant part of African countries still lack access to good, clean, pipe-borne drinking water; effective healthcare is still beyond the reach of a sizeable number of the population in Nigeria; stable electricity in Nigeria is still no-where close to realization; public education is wrought with strikes due to poor and non-payment of teaching staff, thereby affecting our children's future; civil servants find it difficult to cater for their families because the minimum wage cannot take care of their basic needs and at times they are owed salaries, thereby leaving them financially stranded; our police officers, especially the junior officers are not well paid and they have to put their lives on the line to fight crime; our prisons have a lot to do in terms of rehabilitating inmates, our agricultural sector has not fully harnessed the potential of our fertile lands, good climates and numerous crops that can be produced on our grounds; we the African masses have still not learned to effectively put aside our religious, ethnic and tribal differences, so we can work together to implement our basic necessities as a people.

From my experience living in Nigeria, I have noticed that almost all the problems we face in Nigeria and most parts of Africa are man-made problems. Sadly, we are the ones making our lives hard in Africa. We pray to God to bless Nigeria and to bless Africa. Newsflash; God has already blessed Nigeria and Africa with good climate, fertile lands for agriculture, enough manpower in our population, abundant natural resources, magnificent wildlife, among others. Our major problem in Nigeria and Africa are the ones created by our thieving and looting politicians. They are the major reason for our stagnation and even regression in regards to development in Nigeria and in Africa.

Living here in the United States has brought my attention to my African American brothers and sisters. I see great potential among us; the value we add to this great country is beyond words. From academic excellence, to the best sport stars, entertainers, musicians, decent working-class families, among other esteemed contributions; but we are very guilty of shooting ourselves on the foot by the way we treat each other. I believe that change will come, but it has to be from within us before it can reflect on our families, our society, our way of life and collectively on Africa.

In light of this, I have decided to lay down my humble thoughts on what we can do to individually achieve redemption from within, because we cannot give what we don't have and not until we are internally, mentally and psychologically redeemed, we will continue to display those poor traits that has kept us in these mental shackles. I will try to keep this novel as concise as possible.

Please, open your minds and your conscience as you read and hopefully enjoy this novel.

GOVERNMENT

WHAT BETTER PLACE to start? If the head is faulty, the body suffers. Good governance is the major criteria to a successful, progressive and developed community. In light of this, I would continue to lay emphasis on the importance of good governance throughout this book. The Nigerian government is very wealthy as a result of the proceeds the country makes from oil, gas, agriculture, among others. The individuals that are in various leadership and serving positions of government need to start thinking progressively. When we say the country will get better, it has to start from somebody, from people, from the government. A lot of excuses have been given in the past, even until now, on why the government cannot effect positive changes on the lives of the populace.

The answer is not far-fetched. Eschewing corruption alone will produce a massive positive change in the lives of Nigerians and Africans as a whole. Nigerian and African leaders should understand that if our countries are going to look like a place where sane people inhabit, money meant for fixing bad roads and construction of new roads, building numerous hospitals of international standards all across the nation, including rural communities (life has great value), equipping our public primary, secondary and higher institutions with modern laboratories and libraries with books that are part of the syllabus for each class, fixing and erecting traffic lights, zebra crossings and stop signs as appropriate, ensuring our transportation system, postal system, police, military, public school teachers, civil servants are well taken care of, among other public services that ensures a smooth and competent functioning of the community, must be used for these developmental purposes and should have no business being in some crooked individuals' private pockets. Some of these crooked individuals are in places of leadership and in the government and these criminals that perpetrate these selfish, shallow, immature and short-sighted acts are sabotaging the progress and development of Nigeria and Africa as a whole.

Redemption from within is challenging individuals that find themselves in various government positions to forget whatever self-serving reasons they chose to go into political office. Those self-serving reasons that will make a man or a woman in government to divert funds meant for fixing roads, equipping hospitals, schools, bringing electricity and pipe-borne water to rural communities and to the whole of Nigeria 24 hours every day, paying our school teachers and civil servants, providing our policemen with good housing, effective healthcare (life has great value), adequate vehicles, improving the welfare of the populace, and rather using those monies for their own personal benefit, even when all our politicians are already paid exorbitant salaries that will ensure they live comfortably.

The African mind must mature and it is this mental maturity that will make a president, vice-president, senate president, senators, house of representative members, governors, state house of assembly members and the local government to imbibe the habit of accountability, transparency and use public monies for development of the community, thereby empowering the people and greatly improving their welfare. The African mind must be enlightened on the benefit of professional service and accountability to the people. Mental maturity should be a trait that any individual in government possess and those individuals in places of leadership who cannot for the reasons of greed, corruption and self-serving agendas, fathom the importance of mental maturity in regards to using public money for community development, empowering the people and improving their lives, those individuals should be immediately stopped in their criminal and short-sighted tracks, stripped off of the government and leadership position they use as platform to carry out their dysfunctional mentality and locked up in prison where their criminal, greedy and economic sabotaging minds belong. While in prison, they should be rehabilitated, by strictly and comprehensively teaching them through education, how transparency, accountability and good governance can positively affect their community and how embezzling public funds is hurting and destroying their community. Hopefully these shallow-minded economic saboteurs and looters might see the light and change their ways. Hopefully that is.

The government should focus on dispensing service to the people and those criminal elements that hold government and leadership positions and line their pockets with public money should be kicked out of office immediately and whatever monies they embezzled must be recovered from them and injected back into the communities' development where it rightly belongs.

It takes self-discipline and mental maturity for an African public office holder to be contented with their already very good salaries, see monies meant for public development and say to themselves; "This is public money, it must be used to fix my community's roads and create side-walks for pedestrians; this is public money, it must be used to provide pipe-borne water for those communities that lack this essential and basic need of life; this is public money, it must be used to fix the roof of our community's public schools, put good and adequate furniture in the classrooms, equip the laboratories with all the necessary supplies, provide lunch for primary and secondary school children during their break-time hours and having government funds set aside for financial aid for those students from poor homes whose parents cannot afford to send to higher institution, but these students excel in their academics; this is public money, it must be used to provide adequate vehicles for our policemen and policewomen, provide them with lunch, provide them with healthcare, give them the right tools both in technology and weaponry to effectively fight crime, provide each policeman and policewoman with a functioning radio to call for back-up and radio their colleagues from various departments and locations to combine and curb crime, provide clean, beautiful houses both on and off barracks, that are well painted, spacious, has running water, very clean bathrooms and toilets, beautiful recreation centers and sponsoring children of fallen policemen and policewomen through their university education; this is public money, it must be used to purchase more ambulance and emergency vehicles to quickly transport accident victims and victims of medical emergencies that dial our emergency phone numbers (life has great value), this is public money, it must go towards the payment of our public primary, secondary and university teachers and instructors' salaries, because these educators have families to cater for and have earned their wages; this is public money, it must be used to pay civil servants". When an African public office holder can make such a determination from within their minds, the system will start working effectively.

The above I just mentioned may sound funny to minds from developed countries because these are regarded as the basic mindset of a prosperous community and because this mindset has eluded so many individuals in leadership positions in Africa, these basic necessities seem so far from reach. That is why we are still in the man-made predicament we find ourselves in Africa, especially in Nigeria. Until we mature mentally, we will continue to display subhuman traits that make our communities look less human.

What do I mean by subhuman traits? The criminal elements and economic saboteurs that hold public office and use that office as a platform to loot public funds meant for development are displaying subhuman traits through their short-sighted, shallow and immature mentality and their actions have far-reaching consequences into various systems of the country and negatively affects the life of the people; the criminal elements and saboteurs of progress among the police force that collect bribes, harass innocent civilians, are paid money by rich men and women to harass a poor citizen of Nigeria, thereby, going against their pledge to serve and protect the community, the criminal elements among the military that use the platform of the army to harass innocent civilians, beat up civilians for no just cause, have a civilian lay in dirty water, lay in gutters, drink dirty water as punishment for petty offenses, when we have a rule of law under a democratic dispensation, thereby abusing the sacred rights of a Nigerian citizen whom they swore to defend, these criminal individuals are saboteurs to our Nigerian police and Nigerian military and are displaying subhuman traits that have kept and is still keeping Nigeria and Africa in the dark. When criminal elements among the citizens of Nigeria catches a petty thief in this modern era, viciously beats up the suspected thief and burn/lynch the suspected thief alive, we are displaying subhuman traits.

Now, when we step back and look at the manifestations of the impact our collective mentalities have wrought on our communities, do we see the critical and immediate need for us Nigerians and Africans to get mentally matured, or are we going to continue to live in denial and continue in those filthy traits?

The need for we Nigerians and Africans to come to the realization of the massively negative impact that our shallow and greedy mentalities are doing to our communities is very vital. Our youths are leaving in droves to seek a better education and future in foreign countries because they see little to no future in their homelands, as a result of the havoc the criminal elements in positions of government have done to the lives of the people. Our youths are tired of strikes in higher institutions that will prolong a course of four years to six years or more. Our youths are tired of having to 'settle' or sleep with lectures in order to pass, our youths are tired of cultism that have plagued our higher institutions and have seen the wanton destruction of students' lives and properties, our youths are tired of being unemployed and under-employed, our youths are frustrated with the difficulty of getting federal grants to start a business, our youths are feeling left-out and hopeless, with nothing to look forward to in a country like Nigeria that is very rich and blessed with resources. Our youths are tired of living under the bridge as area boys and used as political thugs by criminal elements in our political system that uses these naïve and vulnerable youths by paying them peanuts to disrupt the voting process and ensure they remain in public office, not so they can serve, but to fill their pockets with public money. These saboteurs and criminals have no place in a progressive and modern era and our youths should stop selling their future for peanuts, rather they should demand good leadership and accountability from their leaders and ensure that the law is respected and those criminal elements in political and government positions should be locked up in prison where they belong and their greedy and immature mindsets should be enlightened.

When we as youths accept money from a thieving politician to disrupt the voting process and ensure the criminal stays in office, you are not only hurting yourself and your future, but are also an accomplice by helping that dysfunctional politician to keep Nigeria and Africa in the dark, keep the citizens of Nigeria and our children suffering and impeding the progress of the nation. Have you asked yourselves why we still do not have 24 hours of uninterrupted power supply in Nigeria? Have you asked yourselves why you don't have a bright future in your own country? Have you asked yourselves why you cannot afford life-saving healthcare in your own country? Need I remind you that the masses cannot afford to travel abroad for effective and life-saving healthcare? Do I need to reiterate to we youths that it is only common-sense to have the belief that life has great value? Need I remind we youths that our folks and their children living in areas such as Makoko in Lagos, Ajegunle in Lagos and other parts of Nigeria with inhabitable conditions have 'representatives' in the house and senate? Why should we youths aid the behavior of the criminal elements among the government, by helping them stay in power? Don't you know by such actions you remove any hope left of a better Nigeria, because the belief is that if these present crop of political office holders in government couldn't care less about development and progress as long as their pockets were big with public money, the onus rests on the next generation of Nigerians, which are today's youth, to bring Nigeria into a civilized state in this modern era? We youths need to wake up to our responsibilities of ensuring that Nigeria and Africa move swiftly from its present undesirable state to a developed and civilized nation. **A developed and civilized nation is one where ALL systems of the nation works, leadership is accountable to the people and the rule of law is respected.**

I mentioned about those poor children that are victims of the criminal elements in political and government positions; we as youths, when we see those children, don't you think they deserve to live in a beautiful house, eat healthy and nutritious meals three times a day, have parents that can afford to feed them because leadership is good and food is affordable, live in a clean environment, be adorned in clean and beautiful shirts and shorts and clean shoes, have clean and kempt hair and when you look at them, you smile and say "that's my angel?"; rather, due to a significant number of criminals in political office of government, we have for the most part, the wrong mentalities and these basic common-sense of life eludes them. They are blinded by their greed, selfishness and immature actions, thereby, making life difficult for parents and you get to see scenes like those in Makoko, Ajegunle and many other parts of Nigeria, of our beautiful children, only dressed in dirty underwear, roaming the streets, are hungry because their parents cannot afford three meals a day, looking unkempt and are vulnerable to abuse.

The sad thing is that we tend to have normalized these absurd conditions of living, which makes me seriously question our sanity in Nigeria and in Africa. The status of our living condition is in a critical state and unless our political office holders in government reach within themselves and imbibe the traits of discipline and mental maturity, passing bills and implementing laws that protect the rights of citizens of Nigeria, immediately removing corrupt political office holders, recouping their loot and putting back the recovered resources into the community's development, making the law serve both the rich and poor equally, making the justice system swift and effective, we may continue to wallow in those actions that have left us at the bottom in terms of development.

EMPLOYMENT

LIKE I MENTIONED earlier in this book, I will keep putting emphasis on the importance of good governance, because it is going to take a competent government that is devoid of dysfunctional elements to implement the necessary actions in order for all the systems in the country to work. Providing employment for the populace is part of the responsibilities of our government and when our government eschews corruption, it makes the business clime very good and attractive for investors and the private sector to also help in the creation of jobs.

Providing adequate employment to our large population in Nigeria and in Africa will go a long way to curb criminal activities, because many of our jobless youths that go into terrorism, militancy, kidnapping, armed robbery, oil pipe-line vandalism, area boys, 'omo onile', drug peddlers, fraudsters/ scammers, among other heinous crimes, will be gainfully and legitimately employed, be able to cater for their families and will see little to no need of joining any criminal group to perpetuate despicable acts.

When the government removes all dysfunctional political office holders whose aim is to steal public monies meant for development, the government now places itself in the perfect position to effect development, because funds meant to serve Nigeria and Africa, will do just that, rather than being in the domestic or foreign bank accounts of political thieves.

The Nigerian government and African governments should resolve to create employment by forging partnerships that benefit the people of Nigeria and Africa. These partnerships should include; professional training with skills acquisition in road construction and maintenance, electricity, plumbing, welding, gardening, farming, technology, transportation services, postal services, healthcare, automobile factories, science, building and construction, catering, among other vast community services. The government can partner with experienced professionals locally, continentally and globally, who have excelled in that specific area of training they are going to teach our youths in Nigeria and other parts of Africa.

These skills acquisition are vital for the masses, especially our youths; because when the Nigerian government and other African governments are now filled with mentally matured politicians, after getting rid of the dysfunctional ones, the government can now initiate the process of rebuilding Nigeria and Africa and this is going to require a lot of skill and manpower. Having the Nigerian and African population adequately trained in various fields of the rebuilding process, will ensure they are competent enough to be employed when our bad roads are getting fixed, when we are constructing new roads, bridges and putting up street lights, traffic lights, zebra crossings, pedestrian sidewalks that are also accessible to disabled folks on wheelchairs and putting up foot bridges; when we are putting electricity in our rural areas and supplying power 24/7 all over Nigeria; when we are putting up pipe-borne drinking water all over Nigeria and Africa; when we are building hospitals both in cities and in rural communities that have modern facilities of international standards, so good that our president and masses of Nigeria alike, can go to for basic healthcare and even life-saving healthcare, when we are building new markets and renovating the existing ones that are in very bad condition, such as the Ariaria international market in Aba, Abia state, among others. All of these will require skilled individuals from Nigeria and Africa who will be employed, thereby significantly curbing the problem of unemployment and underemployment.

Good maintenance is the key to ensuring our community continues to look good, decent, developed and functioning. It is only common-sense that whatever we build or fix can be damaged or undergo wear and tear with time, hence the need for ongoing maintenance. We should not be complacent, rather, when we build or fix things, we should imbibe the habit of maintaining them. We want to continuously see our roads looking good and clean, with the lane markings very visible, we want to see all our traffic lights functioning perfectly, we want to see our sidewalks and our lawns in good and clean conditions, we want to see our hospitals continuously maintained and any equipment that gets damaged or worn out, be it a bed, machine, among others, should be replaced within a reasonable time, we want to see our police and military lodges in their barracks always looking clean, beautiful, well-painted, with running water, we want to see our highways, freeways and bridges in good conditions, we want to see our streets clean, with no refuse on the floor, we want to see those untarred and pot-holed filled roads all over Nigeria fixed and maintained, we want to see the grasses on our stadiums looking healthy, green and well graded, we want to see our stadiums well managed, looking beautiful and clean, we want to see our public schools looking well-painted, not built haphazardly with only a half wall and zinc for a roof, thereby leaving our children exposed to the elements during stormy weathers, we want to see good furniture in all our public schools, even in rural areas, so no child has to sit on the floor to learn, we want to see our public bus parks looking clean, decent, with no area boys around to harass drivers and their conductors, we want to see our markets clean, with no refuse on the floor and merchandize sold in healthy conditions, we want to see our airports (both international and local) well managed and in good condition.

Maintenance is the key to keeping our communities in the right path of development, otherwise, every effort we put in towards developing will go to waste. Maintenance of our infrastructure will go a long way to ensuring many Nigerians stay employed and our community looks good while achieving that feat.

SECURITY

L IFE HAS GREAT value. The lives of Nigerians and Africans as a whole are of utmost importance, both poor and rich alike, therefore, safeguarding lives and property should be highly prioritized by the government. A very organized security apparatus is vital for a community to be safe, stable, have social and community order and to be functional. Crimes are perpetuated by people in the community. Effective policing network, can help curb crime to a very good extent.

The government should equip our policemen and policewomen with a functioning vehicle to each team of 4 policemen/women, each policeman/woman that patrol the streets must be provided with a bullet-proof vest when on duty, each policeman/woman, must have a functioning radio that can be used to call for back up when responding to crime, each police officer's vehicle must be equipped with a camera, each policeman/woman must have basic CPR training because our police are not only in the business of protecting lives, but also of saving lives.

Our police departments must be well funded by our federal and state governments to ensure all police departments have modern computerized systems, electronic data, electronic booking and fingerprint systems, a competent and functioning communications system where the public can dial a very short and easy-to-remember emergency number and our police communications system picks it up and radio police patrol units assigned to those surrounding areas to hurry to the distressed location and also radio surrounding police units to hurry there as well for back up and effective curtailment of criminal activity. This should be so even in rural parts of Nigeria. It is a big shame when we see cases of armed robbery that lasted for an hour and no law enforcement showed up or they showed up after the robbers already robbed and left victims dead or injured. That is clearly the result of a failed state. Our security personnel should be able to respond to all distressed areas within 8 minutes. Our fire department should be well equipped with adequate fire trucks and emergency ambulance to hurry alongside our police cars to distressed areas for the immediate transport of injured persons to the hospital. Please, let's start getting the basic things of life right in Nigeria and in Africa. Cameras should be mounted above traffic lights and CCTV cameras should be erected on major streets.

There should be no such thing as vigilante, where a group of rascally youths claim to 'protect' the community, catch a petty suspected thief, viciously beats the suspected thief and burn/lynch them alive, while the community watches these cruel and inhumane actions while hailing and cheering them on. Boy, are we sick in Africa! We Nigerians and Africans seriously need to stop these barbaric, subhuman, shameful and despicable acts of callousness and every perpetrator of jungle justice that leads to the death of a suspect should be charged with murder.

Our police force should be well trained through education

and on the field to curb crime, to be professional, to respect the rights of Nigerians and to be friendly to the communities they are serving. Also, our police force should be paid well; enough to live comfortably. We should have police detectives that are very well trained in the handling of cases, including crime scene and our police departments should have well trained forensics team that are experts at collecting and analyzing evidence from a crime scene. The branch of the police force known as the Special Anti-Robbery Squad (SARS) must be reformed by thoroughly screening this department of the police force and dismissing the miscreants among them that abuse their power by harassing and brutalizing innocent civilians. We have seen cases where a SARS official threatens to shoot a civilian and boasts that nothing will happen. Now, this is a security official sanctioned by the police to protect the lives and properties of Nigerians, but these bad elements are threatening to murder Nigerians and nothing will happen. This is the level of decadence that persists in our security apparatus in Nigeria and Nigerians must demand that all such potential murderers that utilize the platform of SARS to murder Nigerian citizens be dismissed from SARS and prosecuted. Any security official, be it a police officer, soldier, SARS, FRSC, civil defense corps, and so on, that threatens to kill a Nigerian citizen must be arrested and prosecuted immediately!

When Nigeria and Africa expunge dysfunctional, thieving politicians and now have mentally matured public office holders, money meant for the security system in the country will go towards what it was meant for. We will have a well-trained police force that have good communications gadgets and network, adequate police vehicles, swift response to crime, intelligent response to crime in the form of police detectives and forensic experts, well-equipped and very reliable police, very professional police, a police force that is well cared for and we can be proud of.

If these are implemented, we will have very little to no cases of street thugs, jungle justice, cultists clashing with each other and leaving innocent Nigerians dead in the process, thugs and area boys harassing public transport workers and extorting money from them, thugs extorting money from shop and store owners, **marauding Fulani herdsmen that have killed many innocent Nigerians, including children and little to no action have been taken by the Nigerian government to clamp down on them and protect Nigerians from these marauding Fulani herdsmen**, among other numerous social disorders that have plagued Nigeria and African countries for so long. These social disorders are for the most part, the result of having criminal, thieving and looting politicians that have diverted funds budgeted for security, thereby leaving our police heavily underfunded and poorly taken care of to fight crime. **Corrupt, stealing and looting political office holders are the number one obstacle to a successful Nigeria and a successful Africa**. If you don't take to heart anything else from this book, I implore you to seriously consider this biggest, bolded text and act to change this in order to deliver Nigeria and Africa from this man-made predicament we have found ourselves in.

When next you see bad roads, remember the looting politician that has converted money meant for fixing that road for themselves. When next you see our policemen and policewomen poorly dressed, poorly paid, with almost no equipment to fight crime with, remember the looting and thieving politician; when next you see a government hospital with poor and broken-down facilities, remember the thieving and looting politician; when you see our children in public primary and secondary schools sitting on the floor to receive lectures due to broken down furniture in classrooms, remember the looting and thieving politician; when you see your fellow Nigerians and Africans falling victims to rampant kidnappings, robberies, jungle justice, extortion, injustice and what have you, remember the thieving and looting politicians. I hope these few examples out of the numerous meted out there by the dysfunctional ruling system has brought to our attention the number one obstacle of progress in Nigeria. Well, when you think about that, remember the thieving and looting politician that has stashed public money meant for the development of various systems of our community into their own pockets, thereby leaving our communities in disarray.

I stated that I will keep emphasizing on the need for good

governance and how poor leadership is hurting, really hurting development in Nigeria and in Africa.

Securing of lives and property is indicative of a functioning government and country, while a country that records a high rate of cultists, thugs' clashes, marauding Fulani herdsmen attacking and killing people on their farms, killing and maiming people in communities, among other heinous crimes are indicative of a failed state. A failed state is the result of an overall failure of all systems of a nation, due in most part to looting and thieving politicians that have financially crippled the nation, thereby rendering the nation weak to fund the effective curtailment of community and social disorders.

EDUCATION

THE IMPORTANCE OF education cannot be overemphasized. I am really proud of most of our Nigerian and African youths, that despite what we have suffered from our dysfunctional ruling systems, we have persevered and have done exploits in our academics. We have devised means of survival, by leaving our dysfunctional education system at home and going abroad to study in a different clime, far away from family and loved ones, but we strived to be successful at school, because we know the importance of having a good education and the opportunity that it gives to us and to our family.

I have met countless young bright minds at school from Nigeria and from different parts of Africa and it gladdens my heart that we have a lot of African youths, who through the empowerment of education now fully understand what running a developed and progressive community entails.

When we think about this, we can easily see how a government that is mostly infested with thieving and looting politicians couldn't care less about fixing our education system in Nigeria and in Africa, because these dysfunctional elements in political office need a populace that is poorly educated and are slaves to poverty of the mind. They need these sorry minds, because it makes it a lot easier for these dysfunctional politicians to loot our beloved country dry and the people are not enlightened enough to demand accountability and transparency; the people are not enlightened enough to know their rights and to stand up for them, the people are happy to accept crumbs and even hail some of these political criminals, the people are not enlightened enough to understand that not having electricity 24 hours a day is the result of a failed system, rather, they go buy candles, lanterns and generators and continue suffering, while still accepting crumbs and thinking it is okay to live like an animal; the people are not enlightened enough to understand that all the failed systems in Nigeria and in Africa are for the most part, the direct cause of dysfunctional public office holders.

Education is very vital if Nigeria and Africa are going to develop at a pace that is significantly faster than a snail. We want our public primary and secondary schools to be equipped with adequate furniture, so our children don't have to sit on the floor to receive lectures. We want our public primary and secondary schools to be properly built and not the haphazard structures we mostly see around with half walls and a zinc for a roof. This is not how a wealthy country like Nigeria should treat our children, especially in this modern era. Our public primary and secondary schools should not look like a poultry, rather, the environment should inspire learning.

Our public primary and secondary schools should have libraries that contain all the books used in the syllabus for each class, where students that come from poor homes whose parents are not well-to-do and can't afford to buy their children some of the textbooks for their numerous classes, can use the school library books to complete their assignments and to study. The school libraries in public primary and secondary schools should have librarians that keep the library open for at least four hours after school hours for primary and secondary school students that need to use the books from the library to complete assignments and to study. Our public primary and secondary school children should be provided with free and healthy lunch (with the inclusion of fruits) by our government. The implementation of all of these will greatly alleviate the sufferings of civil servants and poor parents, in regards to training their children through school on their little salaries.

Under no circumstances should our teachers in public primary and secondary schools be owed salaries. If we think this is an impossible feat to achieve, I'm encouraging my Nigerian and African public office holders that if we can expunge looting and thieving public office holders from the positions they hold, achieving this feat will be easy as 'ABC', because monies budgeted for teachers' salaries will go towards paying the teachers, rather than being in the personal bank accounts of political looters. See how political thieves are always rearing their heads as our number one obstacle to progress in Nigeria and all over Africa? We seriously need fresh and progressive minds at the helm of affairs to bring Nigeria and the whole of Africa into the modern era of development.

Our higher institutions must be devoid of cultism and other social vices, because our universities and polytechnics should be a place of higher learning where our youths display their bright minds, conduct research, synthesize inventions and modify existing ones, obtain practical learning and not just theory and aspire for the best, thereby producing graduates that are ready for the modern world and are prepared to move Nigeria and Africa to a civilized state.

We don't want any more incidence of cultism in our higher institutions. Adequate security should be provided for our youths in our higher institutions so that they stand very little to no chance of falling victims to cultism. Any dysfunctional youth who decides that being progressive in the mind, learning and using the environment of our higher institution positively, is not their cup of tea and would rather use our higher institution grounds to practice cultism, thuggery, attacking innocent people and being a nuisance, should be immediately arrested by the authorities and prosecuted, so that these dysfunctional minds do not hinder the progress of our higher institutions and make innocent and responsible students victims of their stupidity.

Lectures and instructors from our higher institutions should be progressive and be good mentors to our youths. Those bad eggs among our lecturers that harass and threaten to fail students if the student does not purchase their 'handout' and if the student does not give in to their sexual demands must be reported to the authorities and those bad eggs arrested and prosecuted immediately. Bringing positive change to an environment means that things will no longer be 'business as usual'. Our good lecturers and instructors know those bad colleagues in their ranks that exploit students financially, sexually and otherwise. Our good instructors must act by reporting those bad eggs in their ranks, because when those bad eggs are removed and replaced with good instructors, the system is now changing for the better. Positive change can only happen when good people do the right thing, by stopping the evil ones in their tracks.

We want education empowerment especially for our

vulnerable daughters in the northern part of Nigeria, where the girl child is at risk of child abuse by having them married off to men when they are still minors. The Nigerian government should hastily come to the rescue of these children in the Northern part of Nigeria, by making unconstitutional any marriage to a minor and the adults involved in marrying off that child should be arrested and prosecuted. **The Nigerian law must become reasonable and alive in order to protect its citizens, especially the most vulnerable, who are our children**.

Many years ago, my beloved country of birth, the United States of America, had their significant mistakes as well, when they saw nothing wrong in using Africans as slaves. Today, the United States of America is one of the leading nations in the world when it comes to respecting human rights and protecting minors from predators. The United States has evolved in the right direction by learning from their mistakes.

The Nigerian government can also evolve in the right direction by learning from our mistakes, by understanding in this regard, that there is everything wrong with a grown man preying on the girl child in the name of marriage. The Nigerian government should arise and defend her children from predators. **What the girl child needs is empowerment through education so they can have a bright future and not being child brides to pedophiles.**

ROADS

A SIGNIFICANT NUMBER OF our roads, both in urban and rural areas are death traps. This is how bad the situation is. These bad roads are putting the lives of Nigerians at risk. Some citizens of Nigeria have lost their lives in auto accidents as a result of our poor road conditions. All our roads should be in good condition, our street lights should be functioning, the roads should be well tarred, with no pot-holes.

Maintenance of our roads should be a high priority of our ministry of works. The Nigerian ministry of works should have a functioning website where the public can assist them, by taking photographs of pot-holes they see on our roads and upload them to the website, along with the location, so that our ministry of works can quickly dispatch a work team to that location to have that pot-hole fixed and have that road in good condition within a reasonable time.

This is how a good community works. All hands should be on deck and committed to see our environment looking well catered for, looking like a place where civilized minds inhabit. This suggestion is given in the hope that thieving and looting public office holders would already be removed from the helm of affairs, because this is the only way that money budgeted for fixing our roads and constructing new roads as appropriate is put to the right use, otherwise, the budget for these roads will just serve as an avenue for corrupt politicians to fill their pockets, while our roads remain death traps.

Our street roads should all be in good condition and speed limit signs should be posted on our roads, lane markings should be clear, traffic lights should be functioning, side-walks must be created for pedestrians, this would ensure pedestrians are less likely to be run over by vehicles, thereby, preventing the sad occurrences we have witnessed, where pedestrians walk on the side of the road and have been hit by vehicles, leading to their demise.

Our federal road safety corps should be well equipped with functioning radios and vehicles and should work closely with our traffic wardens and police to ensure our road laws are observed, so Nigerian drivers can have a good experience driving on our roads.

My dear fellow Nigerians, we also share a huge responsibility to keep our roads in good condition. Stop dumping refuse on the streets; it makes the environment an eye-sore, stop dumping refuse in the gutters; those gutters serve as drainage and can get clogged when you dump your refuse in there, that's why we have scenarios where rain falls and the place becomes flooded and the gutters are not draining well because they are clogged with refuse. Redemption from within starts from our individual minds to do things better, to relate better with each other, to stop killing each other, to care for our environment, to respect the lives of our fellow Nigerians, to assist our government create a better Nigeria.

Our government has an enormous responsibility to make Nigeria a developed country, but the government needs our full cooperation to make this a reality, because when the government expunges criminal, looting politicians and replace them with mature minds that have come to implement policies to better our nation, they need the citizens of Nigeria to be free of corruption in their places of business, they need we Nigerians to keep our environment clean and stop dumping refuse on the streets and gutters, they need we Nigerians to stop fighting each other, to stop killing and taking laws into our hands, they need we Nigerians to stop vandalizing oil pipe-lines, to stop stealing power cable lines, to stop committing internet fraud and scams, thereby destroying our sacred image, to stop peddling drugs, to stop killing people and using them for rituals, to stop exhuming human remains and selling the parts, to stop kidnapping, to stop joining terrorist groups, to stop walking our cattle herd on the streets, thereby obstructing traffic, rather cattle herders should convey their livestock properly in trucks and stop impeding traffic and to rear their cattle in ranches and not grazing them on peoples' farms, thereby causing community friction, to stop turning our public bus stops into area boys' hangout centers, to stop all those actions of ours that have destroyed Nigeria and kept Nigeria in the dark, making her look like a nation of insane minds.

Our highways should be maintained. Annual inspections, or inspections as needed, should be done on our bridges and repairs should be prompt. Our ministry of works, just like other arms of government have to be proactive and not reactive to the way we manage all systems of our dear nation, this will ensure our infrastructure are always top of the class.

HEALTHCARE

E VERY CITIZEN OF Nigeria and Africans in general deserve effective and world class healthcare that is affordable. Some effort has been put in this regard, but there is still an awful lot left to be done. Our rural communities and urban areas should all be equipped with a reasonable amount of general hospitals, specialized care, including psychiatric facilities. Even our inmates should not be left out when dispensing effective healthcare.

The private sector can also take advantage of the good business clime that a good functioning government will create and set up world class private hospitals and clinics. The government should greatly value the lives of her citizens and the masses should be able to afford life-saving healthcare.

The government should ensure our healthcare workers

get the best training and our healthcare workers should be very involved with the community, especially our rural areas where they are the most vulnerable to diseases, such as malaria, typhoid, dysentery, polio, among others. There is the belief that a nation's progress is measured by how the most vulnerable are treated.

Our healthcare workers should reach out to the communities and teach preventive care, because prevention is better than cure to begin with. Our folks in the rural communities that are not well educated and tend to make poor health choices should be taught in very simple and practical terms how not having their child vaccinated against polio can lead to paralysis and even death of their child, how not having their children sleep under mosquito nets in rural areas can expose them to malaria, how drinking water that is not boiled or properly treated can lead to typhoid, how having unprotected sex, especially with multiple partners, sharing needles and sharp objects, not putting on gloves when touching blood and body fluids of another person can lead to the contraction of HIV and other blood borne pathogens, how not going for treatment and not completing all the medicine your doctor gave you for that tuberculosis is not only detrimental to your health, but also puts people in your community at risk, how smoking around your children puts your children at risk of respiratory complications due to inhaling second hand smoke, how not taking your medicine as prescribed for your high blood pressure will put you at a risk for stroke, among many other important health teachings.

Being a registered nurse, this one directly hits home. Our Nigerian government should prioritize the health and wellbeing of Nigerians. A holistic approach should be used when caring for our patients. The mental wellbeing of Nigerians, especially our elderly should be taken into consideration. Many Nigerians and Africans have different superstitions and we have seen cases where elderly women were abused by some dysfunctional minds. These elderly women were obviously suffering from dementia, Alzheimer's disease and other mental degenerative diseases that affected their behavior and instead of sending them to an appropriate specialized care facility, these elderly women were labeled 'witches' by the dysfunctional minds in their communities and these elderly women were stripped unclad and beaten.

My fellow healthcare colleagues, we have a lot of work to do in terms of enlightening our fellow Nigerians, so they can understand that the old lady suffering from a mental degenerative illness is not a witch who turned into an owl or a bat to attack them in their sleep and then turn back to a human. We need to educate the naïve and dysfunctional minds amongst the citizens of Nigeria that a human cannot turn into an owl, bat, cat or any other animal. We need to be reasonable and rational in our thoughts and stop abusing the elderly who are too vulnerable and weak to defend themselves.

Please, my Nigerian government, clamp down really hard on any perpetrator that abuses our elderly folks and inflicts injury on them, in the name of beating a witch.

We have also seen cases, especially in the eastern and western parts of Nigeria where children are labeled witches and wizards by their dysfunctional parents and dysfunctional community and these children are starved, beaten, even killed in some instances. The government has so much work to do in protecting the vulnerable people of Nigeria and in Africa, which mostly includes our children, elderly and our disabled folks.

A very long time ago, some parts of Nigeria believed that twin children were evil and when a woman gave birth to twins the children were taken to the forest and left there to die. Thankfully a Scottish missionary by the name of Mary Slessor was able to enlighten our folks that there was nothing wrong with twin children.

Nigeria has progressed from that era, but not far enough; as far as our children are still being labeled as witches and wizards, starved, beaten and sometimes killed, I believe we are still displaying some regressing tendencies in this regard. The dysfunctional minds among our Nigerian folks, as a matter of urgency, needs to be enlightened that children are not witches or wizards and albinos are normal human beings just like you and me.

This is the reason education is of utmost importance, because when the populace is empowered through good education, the mind begins to significantly reason in a rational manner.

Our hospitals should be equipped with modern day facilities

that are always functional. Any equipment that gets defective in our government hospitals should be replaced within a reasonable time. Our private hospitals should also adhere to international and world class standards of care. When a patient is brought to the hospital in a case of an emergency, such as gun shot, stabbing, heart attack, new onset of stroke, respiratory emergencies, among other life-threatening emergencies, the patient must be stabilized immediately before any conversation about hospital registration, money, police form, and so on, as the case may be, is asked. Nigerian doctors and nurses should respect the lives of Nigerians. A very big thank you to those many Nigerian doctors and nurses that put the patients' welfare above anything else. Also, may God's blessings continue to abide with those many Liberian, Sierra Leone, Nigerian and other African doctors and nurses that put their lives on the line during the Ebola outbreak few years ago and greatly reduced the number of casualties through their selfless service. God's blessings on even the foreign doctors and nurses who left the comfort of their developed communities, their family, among others and put their lives on the line to take care of patients during the Ebola outbreak. When they talk about stars and heroes, you are the real stars and heroes, because you sacrificed your comfort and even your lives to ensure that others in various health predicament were well catered for. May the souls of those we lost, both patients and healthcare providers alike, during the Ebola outbreak, rest in perfect peace. To the bad eggs among our doctors and nurses that put money above peoples' lives; a very big shame on you. Life has great value and if doctors and nurses cannot acknowledge this by the way they treat a patient that presents with a life-threatening emergency, by asking for a monetary deposit before they can do anything to save a patient's life, should have no business being in the healthcare profession.

Life has great value and we Nigerians and Africans need to display a civilized approach towards the lives of our fellow Africans. This also extends to my African American folks; not forgetting my Caribbean brothers and sisters and to all Africans all over the world. We can scream 'black lives matter' all we want, but if we continue to shoot each other dead, stab each other, carry out drive-by shootings on each other, engage in tribal, ethnic and religious conflicts that has recorded a staggering amount of deaths of Africans by Africans, then by our actions, we are not displaying a civilized approach towards the lives of our own fellow Africans, then how can you be justified when you say that black lives matter? Action speaks much louder than words and the way we treat each other is exactly how we value each other, regardless of what we say.

Redemption from within is imploring us to take a hard look at ourselves as Africans and see how our own actions are hurting our great continent and how our actions are causing so much man-made problems amidst our land of plenty, good climate, fertile grounds for agriculture, among many other blessings God has given us.

We want to see good hospitals in our rural areas that have all the necessary facilities for proper care, where our pregnant mothers can go for their prenatal care, have safe delivery and continue with their follow up care, our folks in the villages can go for routine healthcare and for live-saving health care; our urban areas should also have more world class healthcare facilities so that our politicians don't have to travel abroad to get good healthcare, rather, they can get the best of care on their home soil in Nigeria. This is why our government needs to expunge corrupt politicians from their ranks so that our dear nation of Nigeria can stop losing billions of naira through looting, rather those monies can be put to work for the Nigerian people. Just imagine what billions of naira that is not being looted can do for the people of Nigeria. The Nigerian government should provide affordable healthcare, so that a lot of Nigerians out there that do not have health coverage at their places of employment can register for government health insurance, thereby being able to afford routine and live-saving healthcare.

Many Nigerian masses cannot afford to travel to the United States, United Kingdom, India, Israel, Germany and many other nations with advanced medical facilities for life-saving healthcare. Unfortunately, most of our Nigerian masses have to make do with our mostly substandard facilities in order to save their lives. We have very competent doctors and nurses in Nigeria and all over Africa, but they need modern day facilities and equipment to function properly.

Our political rulers know that most of our facilities are substandard and instead of channeling good money into turning these facilities into world class healthcare centers to benefit the people of Nigeria, these politicians would rather selfishly fly abroad, get very good world class healthcare for themselves then fly back to Nigeria and continue with their looting routine.

Again, I ask those misguided Nigerian youths, why do you take peanuts from dysfunctional politicians to help keep them in power? A good education will go a long way to enlighten us about the benefit of good governance and how a developed community thrives through accountability, diligence and a significantly corrupt-free environment.

Our fellow Nigerian masses have suffered enough in the hands of looting and thieving politicians. The masses are frustrated and depressed, we now see suicides in Nigeria like we have never seen before. I use this medium to appeal to you my brothers and sisters out there that are feeling so depressed and frustrated with life and the hardship you face every day of your lives, please, do not take your life. When there is life, there is hope. Our hospitals should have suicide hot-lines where people can call and get counseling.

There is a saying that you don't cut off your head to cure a headache. Suicide is not the answer. Challenges is something we all go through in life, though a government filled with people-oriented politicians will go far to alleviate the suffering of our dear Nigerians; so please when that hardship bites you and you begin to think about where your next meal will come from, how you will pay your children's school fees, where you will get the money to treat your elderly father who has suffered a stroke, where you will get the money to pay for your university education and exams, how you will repay all the debt you incurred while trying to feed your family and pay your bills due to non-payment of your salary by the government, among many other challenges; please know that there is still hope.

For those of my fellow Nigerians that find themselves in such predicament, please don't give up, hopefully and soon we will get leaders in Africa and not just opportunists and looters. These leaders will bring Nigeria and Africa into the civilized and modern era, these leaders will create affordable healthcare with world class facilities, these leaders will provide health insurance for Nigerians and for civil servants, their spouse and their children so that both rich and poor families alike can have access to quality and life-saving healthcare, these leaders will make provisions for financial aid for our polytechnic and university students so that our children from poor income families that do well in their academics will not be deprived of obtaining higher education, as this is vital to having a successful future.

For now, while we wait to have good and visionary leaders in Nigeria and in Africa, we may find ourselves still struggling to survive from the day-to-day hardship we find ourselves in. Talk to your religious place of worship for help to assist you when you can't meet up with your daily struggles, talk to friends and family, if worse comes to worst, beg for alms; there are still a lot of kind-hearted Nigerians that will donate money, goods and services to help you. Please, I beg you; do not commit suicide.

Nigerian Airways, Nigerian Postal Service & Transportation

OUR TRANSPORTATION AND mailing services needs to be on par with the modern era. Our airports should be looking in good shape, runways should be intact, the restrooms in our airports should be clean, power supply should be constant in all our airports.

Our Nigerian government should please revive the Nigerian airways. We should have our Nigerian airways flights that would serve both Nigerians and foreigners alike to meet their air transport needs within Nigeria (locally) and internationally. Yes, our Nigerian government should partner with the global community to have our flights serve passengers whose destination lies in their various countries.

Reviving the Nigerian airways will create employment for many Nigerians, by hiring well-trained Nigerian pilots, flight crew, aeroplane maintenance, runway maintenance, airport catering services, airport security, baggage handlers, airport cleaning maintenance services, among other airport personnel required to have a functioning airport. This will be a win-win for the Nigerian government, because while providing jobs for the populace through this avenue, they will also make profit from the air transport services that they offer to both Nigerians and to foreigners.

Our Nigerian postal service should come alive again and we the people of Nigeria should be able to send mails from one end of Nigeria to another end of Nigeria. For instance; our folks living in urban cities such as Lagos or Abuja should be able to deliver mail using our Nigerian postal service that can be delivered to even villages in Abia state, Ebonyi state, Cross River state, Osun state, Kano state, Plateau state, among others. You get the point. Our Nigerian postal service should be well funded by the federal government and should serve all locations of Nigeria, both urban and rural areas alike.

The federal government should establish adequate postal service locations that are well funded with vans for delivery, employees that will be hired, thereby serving as an avenue to reduce the high unemployment rate, maintenance crew, among other important postal service personnel.

We are in the modern era where phones and an internet connection can be used for quick delivery of messages, but the postal system will come in handy for mailing important goods to family, friends and loved ones that are in a different location from us in Nigeria. For instance; a young man or woman that have their aged parents living in the village; these folks can buy their old parent's medication prescriptions, among other useful items for their parents and mail them through our postal service. This is where transparency and a system free of corruption is vital, because we do not want to witness scenarios where corrupt postal workers steal peoples' packages and take the contents for themselves. We Nigerians and Africans as a whole have to start displaying a civilized mentality in order for our communities to function well.

Our transportation systems should come alive as well.

Please let's invest some more on our railway systems and partner with some advanced nations to procure modern-day computerized trains that run both intercity and interstate. I know the government of Nigeria is trying to do something in this regard, but is still nowhere close to what we can achieve as a nation if we put in more effort and eschew corruption.

Building and maintaining our train tracks will ensure the employment of a significant number of Nigerians because building a nation in all aspects requires skill and manpower, this is why the citizens of Nigeria and Africans alike should be empowered by our various governments through education and skills' acquisition. Please, let's start getting the basic things of life right in Nigeria and in Africa. This will make our lives a lot easier.

Our buses should be neat and in good condition. Our bus parks and bus stops should not be a haven for area boys and other types of miscreants and extortionists, rather our bus stops and bus parks should be clean, with the buses properly parked and the vicinity welcoming to passengers. Please, let's deviate from the social disorders we are so accustomed to in Nigeria and all over Africa, those social disorders that have made decent minds question our sanity and our ability to successfully self-govern.

NIGERIANS & FELLOW AFRICANS

P LEASE, LET'S WAKE up my fellow Nigerians. Nigeria is a sleeping giant in the sense that it has the resources, manpower and potential at its disposal to become an advanced nation, but unfortunately the resources we have are not being used to bring Nigeria into a civilized state, rather, most of these resources are being squandered by immature mentalities, mostly in our ruling class.

Nigeria needs to wake up and lead our great nation and other parts of Africa out of the dark and into a civilized state. Come on, the days are going by quickly and we have a lot of catching up to do, but we still seem to have no direction, let alone trying to catch up. Let's stop dancing around the circle of failure and build the will and determination to forge ahead.

How can we forge ahead? Expunging institutionalized corruption is a great start. Once corruption is out the window, Nigerians can use its resources to empower its citizens. The leaders of Nigeria will be visionary and people-oriented. The leaders of Nigeria will create a wonderful atmosphere for Nigerians to reside and enjoy. Nigerians will now be able to afford food to feed their children, Nigerians will have health insurance and be able to afford routine and live-saving healthcare in our world-class hospitals that our visionary leaders will create, Nigerians will be able to afford to further their studies in our higher institutions because our visionary leaders will make provisions for financial aid to poor-income families that qualify based on their earnings, our children in public primary and secondary schools will be provided with nutritious lunch (with the inclusion of fruits) during their lunch break, our universities will be devoid of cultism, because our youths will start thinking positively and progressively, our public primary, secondary schools and university teachers will be paid their salaries on time, civil servants will be paid a living wage and will not be owed salaries, we will stop grown men from practicing their pedophile tendencies in the name of marriage to our minor daughters, we will stop accusing our children of witchcraft, beating, starving and killing them, we will stop accusing our elderly, especially our elderly women of witchcraft, stripping them unclad and beating them, we will stop beating and burning/lynching alive our fellow Nigerians that have erred on the side of the law, rather, we will let the law take its course.

To forge ahead, our policemen and policewomen will stop taking bribes, our government will take good care of our police force, provide them with health insurance, provide them with lunch, paid vacation and other good incentives that help boost morale, the children of fallen policemen and women would have their schooling expenses covered by the state up till their university education and the stipends of the fallen officer should be paid in a timely fashion. I feel sorry for the Nigerian police because these brave men and women work in the worst conditions you can imagine. Some of their barracks are worse than poultries, they are short on vehicles, they lack the required technology, gadgets, self-protective gear and weaponry in adequate supply, but this men and women put their lives on the line daily to ensure the safety of Nigerians. Of course, there are bad eggs among the police force whose actions will make you question the notion that police are your friends; but over-all I think we have been a bit harsh on how we judge the Nigerian police in general given the terrible conditions under which they carry out their duties.

To forge ahead, the rights of Nigerians must be respected; any soldier that uses the platform of the military to harass innocent civilians should be arrested immediately and prosecuted, we will become a nation of laws and no longer be a lawless country with a lot of insane and dysfunctional minds, our roads will be well tarred, smooth, free of pot-holes, would no longer look like death traps, our gutters will be clean and free of clogs, we will have electricity supply 24 hours every day, urban and rural communities will have close access to clean, healthy, pipe-borne water, our hospitals will be equipped with modern facilities, both in urban and rural areas, our tourism industry will boom with foreigners coming to get a feel of our good life and culture, our farmers will get the necessary help they need in finance and crops to plant, our agricultural sector will flourish with adequate and healthy crops and livestock to feed our large population in Nigeria and have surplus, thereby making food very affordable, which in turn eradicates hunger from Africa; and Nigerian and African parents can have more than enough to feed their children, thereby not having to rely on foreign aid from the UN and advanced nations to quell the hunger and starvation of African children.

To forge ahead, every citizen of Nigeria should be equal in the eyes of the law, both rich and poor alike. The justice system should not let the rich use their resources to influence the law. The law must be interpreted correctly to all citizens of Nigeria regardless of status. To forge ahead, we as Nigerians and Africans must immediately stop killing each other. The same goes to my brothers and sisters in Somalia, Sudan and other war-torn countries. For how long? For how long are we going to keep living like savages, killing each other and leaving our children as the worst victims of war as they starve and die due to our immature way of settling our differences. Advanced nations also have differences, but don't use it as a platform to fight and kill each other, rather they iron out their differences through constructive dialogue and finding mutual compromise. That is how civilized minds reason. We have to stop using religion, ethnicity and tribalism to divide each other, because these are the tools the dysfunctional elements in government use to keep the masses divided while they loot and plunder your future away. Nigerians from all works of life are victims of bad leadership from corrupt political elements, so why don't we unite through the suffering that we share, irrespective of our tribe to demand for a better way of life?

To forge ahead, the government will have accountable political office holders, become mentally matured and focus on dispensing service to the people, rather than lining up their pockets with public money. Hopefully, the government would have removed the bad eggs from their ranks that reason through their greed and selfishness and couldn't care less if the whole of Nigeria and Africa burned to the ground because of their reckless, mindless and shameless looting.

To forge ahead, prison inmates would be rehabilitated to greatly reduce recidivism, if we are to effectively fight crime, those that have paid their debt to society should be given a second chance. Justice should be swift and fair to all, regardless of status. This will serve as deterrent to would-be criminals.

If we as Nigerians and Africans develop the will and determination to reach within ourselves and reason maturely, all those negative traits that we have previously exhibited that have made Africa the undesirable place it is at present will be replaced with a mentality that is progressive. This progressive mentality that we embrace will reflect positively on our lives and our society. We will stop recording cases of African migrants fleeing severe suffering in Africa, due to bad leadership and risking their lives through the deserts of North Africa and sailing in small boats to Europe. Your lives may have meant nothing to your leaders that squandered your resources, living you in such a hopeless condition, but your lives were of great value to those of us that understand the real value of a human life and its relationship to a successful community and may God comfort your families. May the souls of our African brothers and sisters that have lost their lives in the deserts of North Africa and in the Mediterranean

Sea, trying to escape the suffering and hardship in Africa rest in perfect peace, Amen.

To the masses of Nigeria and Africa, you play a bigger role in bringing Nigeria and Africa to the civilized world. You hold the power to transform Africa into an advanced continent, because the ruling body work for you and you can through your votes remove them if they do not effectively deliver the dividends of democracy and positive change on your lives.

This is why the masses need to wake up and put their religious, ethnic and tribal differences aside. The masses need to know their worth and the power they have to transform their own destinies for the better. Bad leaders for the most part are the reflections of most of the mentalities in that community. It is sad and shameful that some citizens of Nigeria worship looting politicians. A former governor of a state in the southern part of Nigeria was convicted of financial crimes in the United Kingdom, after spending time in prison for his crime, he returned to Nigeria and was hailed by some dysfunctional minds in his hometown who consider this dysfunctional politician to be a hero. We also have present political rulers in Nigeria that have been indicted by the Economic and Financial Crimes Commission (EFCC) of embezzlement, but these criminal elements still remain in office. Why is this so? In a sane clime, these dysfunctional elements would be made to resign immediately and prosecuted, but in Nigeria and in Africa, we continuously fail to get it right. How then can we grow as a people if we continue to allow criminals occupy public office? How are we ever going to develop? How?

Our mentalities in Nigeria and in Africa has to change; both the political rulers and the masses alike, because institutionalized corruption is rapidly burying Nigeria and Africa as a whole and the result is the societal decadence that is glaringly visible on our dilapidated roads, poor hospital facilities, cultism plagued higher institutions, human rights abusing soldiers, epileptic power supply, impoverished populace, broken down infrastructure, high cost of food, high unemployment and underemployment, bribery, extortion of commercial bus drivers and store owners by miscreants, extortion of house builders by the so-called 'omo onile' criminals, jungle justice, kidnapping, high rate of armed robbery that has cut short the lives of many innocent Nigerians, internet fraudsters and scammers, ritualists, 'one-chance' vehicle operators, marauding Fulani herdsmen that have taken the lives of many Nigerian men, women and children and still have not been checkmated by the Nigerian government, among many other social ills that are part of the routine way of life in Nigeria. How can we live like this my fellow Nigerians? This dysfunctional routine way of life, due to bad leadership and followership as a result of our immature mentalities is what has left Nigeria and Africa at the bottom in development and achieving a civilized and progressive state.

My love for my fellow Nigerians and Africans as a whole is what compels me to call us out on our mistakes because the first step to solving a problem is to acknowledge the problem abounds. I feel ashamed when I see the numerous social disorders that thrives in Nigeria and all over Africa, when I see my fellow Nigerians deriving joy in beating and lynching a suspect to death, I cringe in shame, because I know their jovial display of savagery does not reflect the civilized minds among the people of Nigeria, when I see cases of soldiers using the platform of the military to brutalize innocent civilians, I know that there are decent and gallant soldiers out there that are worthy of the Nigerian military uniform that do not share the thuggery and bullying attitude of their dysfunctional counterparts, when I see cases of our political leaders that loot absurd amounts of money, I know there has to be at least one decent African, people-oriented politician out there.

We cannot continue in our 'business as usual' way of doing things in Nigeria, because this present routine is literally killing the people of Nigeria. We as a people have to come to that point in our nation when we stop giving excuses, stop blaming past governments; a new government comes in and blames the previous government but also changes nothing themselves, rather the looting continues in their administration. We have danced around this circle of failure for so long. Redemption from within is telling us it is now time to reach within ourselves and make that determination now to change our mentalities as a people. We have to take the bull by the horn; address problems directly. There are bad roads; send funds IMMEDIATELY and fix those roads to perfection, without considering religion, ethnicity, tribe, or political affiliation and without unnecessary committees and bureaucracy that only serve as an avenue for looters!

Our hospitals lack modern day facilities, IMMEDIATELY procure world-class facilities and equip all our government hospitals both in rural and urban areas alike. The lives of Nigerians are at stake here and while the political class are politicizing this urgent issue, Nigerians are dying. So sad!

Electricity supply is epileptic in this modern era; channel funds and partner with advanced nations of the world to help Nigeria produce enough power to supply all parts of Nigeria with electricity 24hours a day. Many of these developed nations have land areas that are much bigger than that of Nigeria and they can still supply uninterrupted power to their populace. This will be a walk in the park for these developed nations, hence, our need to work with them to assist us. Please, let's forge partnerships with advanced nations of the world to come and rescue Nigeria from her electric woes. When you have a problem, you should not be ashamed to ask for help, because pretending that everything is fine will only leave the people of Nigeria suffering while you put a false front to the global community. **Asking for help means you are wise enough to know that the predicament you are in can be better solved with more heads than one.**

When electricity supply becomes stable in Nigeria, I can guarantee the Nigerian government that they would have solved unemployment in a very massive scale than they can imagine, because many Nigerians that run small scale businesses and have to spend significant thousands of naira a week to fuel their generators will save that money and instead inject that capital directly into their business to produce better dividends. Our youths and grown folks alike can now successfully run barbing and beauty salons, copy centers and business services, laundry centers, tailoring services, making and selling ice-cream, gaming centers, football viewing centers, grain processing and milling services, bakery, fish ponds, thereby being able to supply fish to local markets, among many other small scale, but thriving businesses that requires constant electricity to flourish.

Please, let's move, giddy up and get to work. There is so

much work to be done in Nigeria and all over Africa. The state of our situation is critical and we have to treat it like the emergency that it is. Dysfunctional public office holders should be removed ASAP and Nigeria should immediately initiate the process of rebuilding, because there is no more time to waste. The modern era is here! The modern era is here! I repeat to my fellow Nigerians and Africans; we are in the modern era! We cannot continue to remain in the medieval times; with poor electricity, public lynching, mindless killing of each other like savages, marrying underaged girls, starving, beating children and accusing them of witchcraft, dilapidated roads and public schools, among other poor infrastructure. Africans, please let's wake up and achieve our great potential.

Remember our stay on earth is only a passing phase. Let's use it wisely to make our lives, our community and the people of Nigeria and Africa a lot better; this way, we leave a developed Africa for our children to inherit and continue in the direction of progress. It will be a happy day in Nigeria and in Africa, when the masses can afford live-saving healthcare, because the government has created affordable health insurance and established a lot of world-class hospitals, when our roads are looking very smooth and beautiful, when we have electricity supply 24 hours every day, when food is very affordable, thereby ensuring our children do not go hungry, when the true beauty of the African mind reflects on how civilized we become in how we interact with one another and constructively resolve our differences, when our matured mentality reflects on the beauty of our environment and our way of life. I eagerly look forward to that day and earnestly hope it materializes in our lifetime. **For the record my African brothers and sisters, the motherland is not a 'sh..hole', rather, the motherland is passing through a challenging and trying state brought about by the wrong mentalities and what we have to do as good children of the motherland is to work on improving our collective mentalities and I can assure you that the more we positively adjust our mentality, the more the beauty of the motherland begins to radiate. God bless Africa, God bless our Haitian brothers and sisters.** Please my fellow Africans, read Revelation chapter 3 verse 19.

AFRICAN AMERICANS

S TRONG, LIVELY, STYLISH, fun to hang around with, brave, played a huge part in building the United States and making her the economic successful country she is today. The exploits of the United States of America have been made possible, to a significant part, by the role played by various African American folks who ensured African Americans were treated fairly and could equally achieve the American dream based on the content of their character and not by the color of their skin, which by the way is awesome!

As African Americans, we have to go back to the drawing board on how to solve our issues. Nobody is perfect, but there is so much work to be done within our community to significantly straighten our path.

When I speak of going back to the drawing board, I am talking about getting it right from the family unit. **A populace that is morally healthy is based on a successful family unit**. In light of this, we as African Americans should strengthen our family ties. When our family ties are strong, our children grow in a healthy environment; parents ensure their children are respectful, hardworking, disciplined, responsible, obey the law, are not self-centered, possess good work ethic, among other positive social traits.

Our children should not be raised in broken homes. What do I consider a broken home? Any home where a child is deprived of love and care from both parents or even one of the parent, due to the father or mother spending most of their time at work and having little to no time to raise their child/children, one or both parents smoke in the house, thereby exposing the child to second-hand smoke, parents doing drugs, smoking and taking drugs while pregnant, incarceration of the father or mother, domestic abuse, especially when witnessed by the children, verbally, physically and emotionally abusing your children, using vulgar language around children, children growing up around drugs, guns and gang violence, not properly feeding your children and not giving children the healthcare that they need, among other dysfunctional parenting styles that can harm a child's physical, psychological and emotional growth. These are what I consider to be a dysfunctional environment for our children.

To our African American youths, the power for a better future is in your hands. The United States of America is still the greatest country on the planet at this time, despite not being perfect and we have the capacity within us to lead better lives. To we African American youths, our country provides us with opportunities we may not get living anywhere else in the world. I'm speaking from experience and I also believe a lot of people feel this way, otherwise, how do you explain the influx of immigrants from around the globe to the United States?

Let us work on our character to help shape a new way if needed, to ensure our future is better than our past and even present. The onus rests on us to make our path more straighten for our children. Some of us may have grown up without our fathers or mothers in our lives, due to many issues. Some of these issues border on weak family ties that stems from poor relationship decisions that degenerated to a dysfunctional family unit, where one parent, especially the father was not very much around and the mother had to struggle with raising the children by herself amid the hassle of working to provide for her children. We know that it takes a community/village to raise a child and not having the father around is one of some of the reasons that weaken family ties and proper upbringing.

Let us cultivate the habit of being there for our children. Even for those men and women that have made relationship decisions to have children with different men and different women (the baby mama/daddy effect), please ensure to be present in your child/children's lives and not just by paying child support, but by being **committed** physically and emotionally to their development.

A committed parental relationship with the child/children begets love to our children, which begets trust from our children to us as parents, which begets a healthy nurturing of our children. When our children are properly nurtured, they for the most part, possess the qualities of discipline, respect for their fellow individual, respect for lives and properties of others, respect for the law, matured enough to seek redress for grievances through the legal channel and through peaceful protests and relentless voicing of our valid concerns and not through violence. When our children are properly nurtured, it will go a long way to break the cycle of bringing up the next generation of African Americans in broken homes. If implemented, we will very much likely see a significant improvement on how we treat each other, we will see little to no cases of our African American brothers and sisters breaking into stores to loot during a hurricane storm (kudos to the brave African American folks who came to the rescue of hurricane Harvey victims, by providing supplies, shelter and other necessities to the victims of Harvey), we will see a drastic decrease of the number of our young men that end up in prison, due to exhibited traits that mostly stems from poor upbringing, this will include; a drastic decrease in African Americans committing black on black crime, huge decrease in thugs killing each other in Chicago, rather, we will have decent and matured thinking African American youths that contribute meaningfully to their family and to society. **Remember that thugs are the end product of a failed family unit.**

Why would a young African American get into a car with his crew with the purpose of driving by and shooting dead his fellow young African American? Why would a young African American shoot dead his fellow young African American because they got into an argument? **Why would a young African American use the N word to refer to their fellow young African American?** The mentality needs to change from the savage, crude, mental faculty, into one that is mature in regards to how we resolve our issues without spilling the blood of our fellow brother. **Life has great value and if we as African Americans do not respect this fact towards each other, we have no leg to stand on when we scream 'Black Lives Matter'.** Even as I keep writing about these issues, I just saw on the local news today 1/31/2018, on *'FOX26'*, a story about a teenager that was shot dead. The police released footage of two suspects, one of whom was an African American teenager and the other probably a teenager of Hispanic descent. This is how bad the situation has gotten; when teenagers kill their fellow teenager without remorse, goes a long way to highlight the **huge** failure in our family unit. When our teenagers go around with a gun to shoot dead their fellow teenager, pretty much shows how bad our situation has deteriorated. Fathers not in their children's lives, single mothers left to bear the enormous task of raising the children and they go to work to earn a living, leaving these kids with little to no nurturing, these kids grow up in such a dysfunctional setting of lack of love, care and nurturing and they turn to their peers whom mostly stem from the same sorry setting, together these young and immature minds make poor decisions by indulging in drugs, joining criminal gangs, having no respect for lives and properties of others, having a hatred for law enforcement, blaming everyone else for their troubles, getting in and out of jail, thereby ruining their chances of securing a good job and worst of all, towing the same destructive path their parents towed, by also having different children by different men and women and not taking the time to nurture them to a healthy mental, psychological and emotional development, thus, continuing the evil circle of broken and dysfunctional family unit. **Getting it right from the family unit is very vital for the progress of the African mind!**

Parents must be positively engaged in their children's lives in order to guide our young brothers and sisters on the right path. To our African American parents and youths alike, let us work on our mentalities and on our character. I will encourage us to be determined in our decision to improve on our character; determined because it is not going to be easy. We may have cultivated bad habits we struggle to break away from. Obstacles are going to be in the way and we need all the help to overcome our demons in order to successfully transform our character.

If your obstacle is a drug addiction, please get help and be genuinely committed to getting rehabilitated. I'm sure you must be aware that you can't secure a decent job or any job at all if you fail a drug screen when you go to get hired. Sometime ago, while I used to work for Walmart, one of the biggest retailers in the United States, my manager used to request I leave my department to help our general merchandize associates unload the truck on time, because at the time, we mostly did not have enough manpower in the unloading area. I once asked a manager why enough hands were not employed back there and was told most of the applicants could not pass a drug test. The drug addiction problem in our country is real and I believe it's also affecting a good number of our African American youths. To all African American youths that have a drug problem, please seek help for this problem, because drug addiction robs you of the opportunity to even start from a humble beginning, such as earning a little, but legitimate income and having a job that although small, serves as a platform for you to advance in a big and established company as a manager and move up in life. Attend your rehabilitation program and commit to it. Consider changing the wrong 'friends' for people that actually care about your welfare, good health and development in life. If you think about what's cool, think about having a clear head devoid of dope and how awesome it is to be in good health due to the decision you took to take control of your life and not be a slave to the demon of drug addiction. If your obstacle is lack of a high-school diploma that may have left you stuck in dead-end jobs, it is not too late to get your GED, there are educational programs, some of them in community colleges that are geared towards helping you get your GED, get into a community college to complete your junior college and move on to a four-year university. This great country has made provisions for financial aid to low income earners.

Only he or she who puts on the shoe knows where it pinches. If life's travails have taken its toll on you, due to poverty, leaving in a dysfunctional family setting where you get no love or care, leaving in a community that only offers you drugs, violence, corpses of folks gunned down by the very social menace and decadence I have been writing about, domestic abuse, discrimination and racism, being unable to seek proper medical attention because you are a drug addict and can't get a job, therefore, can't get health insurance to treat the health complications from drug abuse and you wallow in physiological and psychological pain, you see no hope, therefore delve deeper into self-destruction, you have lost all hope for a bright future and believe you have nothing else to lose, you are depressed; I have words of encouragement for you. *"Earth has no sorrow that heaven cannot heal" – Thomas Moore.*

Our religious places of worship, in addition to non-governmental programs that are geared towards the welfare of our youths need to come to the rescue of our hurting youths. We see them hanging around joints smoking weed, idling about, looking around as people walk by, but we don't know what goes on in their young minds, but we can see their countenance, which is one of hope for a bright future that is lost. We need to serve as a shoulder for our troubled youths to lean on. **Listen to them voice their concerns**, help them in their time of predicament, discipline them with one hand if need be, but don't fail to cuddle them with the other hand. This also applies to the law, I implore our laws to focus on rehabilitating our youths that have erred in the eyes of the law, by helping them learn skills, giving them a second chance in life so they can apply the skills learned to earn a decent and legitimate living, thereby, significantly reducing recidivism. This transcends beyond African American youths. You will be amazed the skills these young men and women possess. No individual with a functioning breath is beyond redemption. Our youths that towed destructive paths did not get the psychological help they needed on time. This is why our religious places of worship, including non-governmental organizations should take up the challenge of reaching out to our troubled youths, showing them love, care, teaching them skills to succeed in life, so that in turn, these youths would no longer be troubled youths, but become rescued, victorious, blessed, cool and awesome youths that now approach life with confidence, now possess the ability to love, care and succeed in life, because they now have these attributes bestowed on them. You can't give what you don't have, but can give everything you have. Therefore, **we should not expect our troubled youths to change if we don't change the conditions that put them in the troubled state they found themselves in.**

The way forward to ensuring our youths' growth is devoid of troubled upbringing is to start getting it right from the family unit. I implore us African Americans to seriously consider this.

There are many problems, challenges, obstacles or personal demons people deal with that may affect their standard of living and even their behavior. Please learn to share your problems with matured thinking folks so you can get help. Remember that a problem shared is one half-solved already. We want to see a lot more of our young African Americans in schools doing well, being good members of society, excelling in sports, difficult finding African Americans in prisons as cellmates because they lead responsible lives, not seeing our young men hanging around bars and joints idling about while their counterparts are at work earning a living and providing for their families.

We may have a lot of excuses and a lot of people that we want to blame, but the ultimate responsibility for our progress or failure in life rests on our shoulders. My fellow African Americans, it is my belief that one day, our communities will have no semblance to a ghetto, we will stop recording black on black killings, we will value the lives of each other, we will get help for our problems, we will show love, care and consideration for our fellow folks, we will spend our time making our communities better, we will take responsibility for our actions, our numbers will be scant in our prisons, our men will be fathers to their children and our women will be mothers to their children, thereby strengthening our family unit and giving our children a bright future. To our numerous African Americans that tread the path of self-discipline, hard-work, are upstanding citizens of this great country, have achieved success through diligence, discipline and a good work ethic, have raised our children with love, care and with a good direction in life, I say great kudos to your efforts and I implore us not to forget our brothers and sisters that may be struggling to grasp these concepts of living, rather, let us through our lives as a living example show them the right path.

May God's blessings and love overshadow our imperfect lives, so that his beauty and light can radiate in our lives, which in turn will radiate in our communities and on how we treat and relate with each other.

AFRICAN POEM

The young men on the farms harvesting yams,

the old men cluttering on bamboo chairs and

speaking of their youth amid drinking from

gourds of palm-wine;

The women tying wrappers and pounding

bush mango with mortars and pestles,

the young girls joggling with pebbles, fetching

water, and assisting their mother with the

cooking;

The boys shooting catapults at birds,

rodents, and sometimes, at each other; reminds

me of the nature land, the mother land; Africa.

By Ifeanyichukwu Uko

www.ingramcontent.com/pod-product-compliance
Lightning Source LLC
Chambersburg PA
CBHW032029290526
45786CB00011B/1192